Silent Night

The Song and Its Story

Silent Night

Written by

Margaret Hodges

Illustrated by

Tim Ladwig

Eerdmans Books for Young Readers

Grand Rapids, Michigan / Cambridge, U.K.

Published 1997 by Eerdmans Books for Young Readers
an imprint of Wm. B. Eerdmans Publishing Co.
255 Jefferson Ave. S.E.,
Grand Rapids, Michigan 49503
P.O. Box 163, Cambridge CB3 9PU U.K.

Printed in Hong Kong

12/01

01 02 03 04 05 06   8 7 6 5 4 3

Library of Congress Cataloguing-in-Publication Data

Hodges, Margaret
Silent night: the song and its story
written by Margaret Hodges; illustrated by Tim Ladwig
unp. p.   cm. : col. ill.
Summary: Tells how the well-known Christmas carol
"Silent night" first came to be written
and performed in Austria in the early 1800s.
ISBN 0-8028-5227-0 (alk. paper)
1. Gruber, Franz Xaver, 1787-1863,
Stille Nacht, heilige Nacht.
1. Gruber, Franz Xaver, 1787-1863.
Silent night, holy night. 2. Mohr, Joseph,
1792-1848. Silent night, holy night.
3. Carols — History and criticism.
I. Ladwig, Tim. ill. II. Title
ML3930.G84H63 2001 1997
782.28' 1723 — dc21
2001023910

The text type is set in Bernhard Modern.
The display type is set in Recklman.
The book was designed by Joy Chu.

For carolers — M.H.

For Briana Noelle — T.L.

It was Christmas Eve,
December 24, 1818, in the old Austrian village
of Oberndorf. All through the valley, children were
counting the hours. Tonight they could stay up late to
go to church for the Christmas service.

Families would come on foot or on sleds, carrying torches and singing, making their way down frozen trails through the snowy pine forests of the lower mountain slopes. The church of St. Nicholas could be seen from a long way off. It was a small church, but above its steeply slanting roof rose the bell tower with its spire pointing to heaven.

As dusk fell, Father Joseph Mohr, a young assistant priest, sat at his desk, working on his sermon. He was gloomy because a big problem had developed that afternoon.

The village choir of boys and girls had come to rehearse their glorious Christmas music. But when Franz Gruber, the part-time organist, had pumped the organ pedals, there was nothing but a wheeze.

The choir members had looked at Herr Gruber in dismay. "Well, friends," he had said, "it seems we must celebrate our Christmas Mass without music. You have worked long and hard to learn your parts. But for this solemn music, the organ must do its part too, and it has broken down. I am very sorry." The children of the choir had gone to their homes, much disappointed.

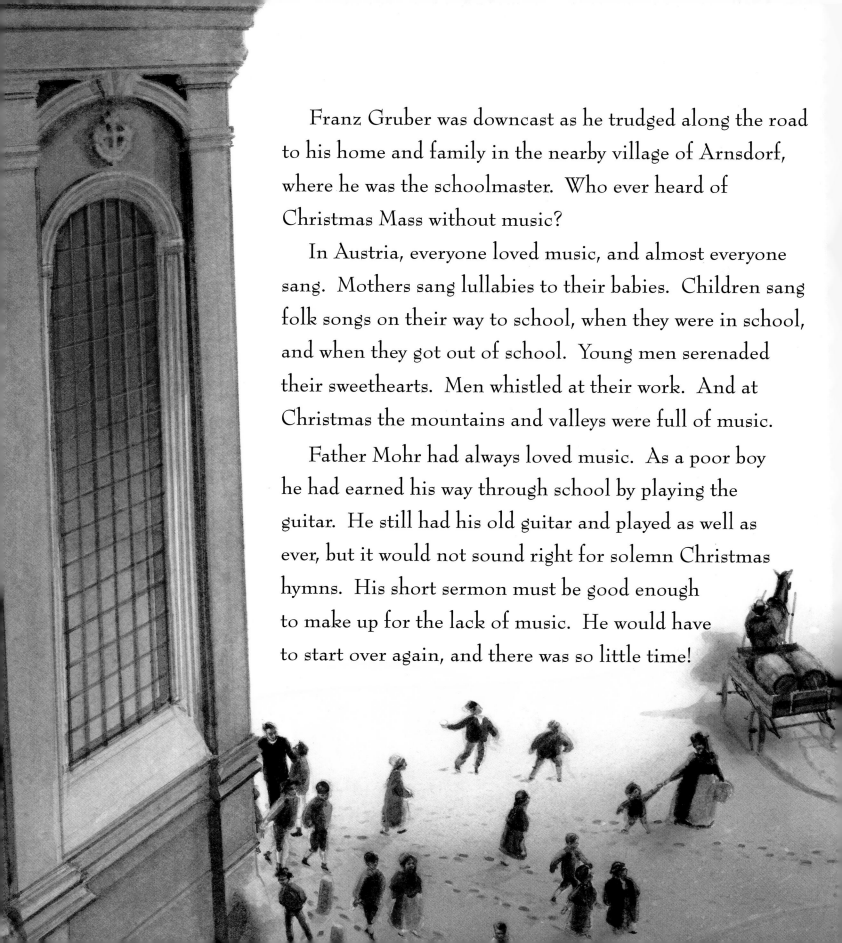

Franz Gruber was downcast as he trudged along the road to his home and family in the nearby village of Arnsdorf, where he was the schoolmaster. Who ever heard of Christmas Mass without music?

In Austria, everyone loved music, and almost everyone sang. Mothers sang lullabies to their babies. Children sang folk songs on their way to school, when they were in school, and when they got out of school. Young men serenaded their sweethearts. Men whistled at their work. And at Christmas the mountains and valleys were full of music.

Father Mohr had always loved music. As a poor boy he had earned his way through school by playing the guitar. He still had his old guitar and played as well as ever, but it would not sound right for solemn Christmas hymns. His short sermon must be good enough to make up for the lack of music. He would have to start over again, and there was so little time!

His small room in the cramped house of the church sexton was stuffy, so he got up and opened his door to get a breath of fresh air. The snow-covered valley lay silent under the stars, the same stars that had shone down on the stable in Bethlehem. Could he write anything as beautiful as the story of how shepherds in the fields, watching over their flocks by night, saw a glorious light in the dark sky, an angel who told them not to be afraid? The angel announced that a baby had been born in Bethlehem and was wrapped in swaddling clothes, lying in the manger of a stable. And this baby was the Son of God, born to save His people. Then a multitude of angels filled the sky, praising God and saying, "Glory to God in the highest, and on earth, peace and good will to all." The shepherds had hurried to Bethlehem and found the baby, just as the angel had said. Mary and Joseph had watched over Him tenderly, and so had the humble animals of the stable.

Father Mohr closed his door and sat down again at his desk.
Perhaps he might write a little song, something as simple as the Bible
story, something that every child could understand. If he could find
the right words, it might not be too late to hurry to Arnsdorf and ask
Franz Gruber to compose an easy tune, like a folk song. Joseph
Mohr picked up his quill pen and began to write in German: "Stille
Nacht, Heilige Nacht. . . ." Silent night, holy night. . . . He wrote six
verses.

When he had finished, he threw on his cape and hurried off
along the snow-covered road to Arnsdorf. Lights shone out
cheerfully from the rooms above the school, where the Gruber family
lived.

Candles gleamed on every branch of the Grubers' Christmas tree, and beneath it lay the presents the children had opened — wooden dolls for the girls, carved by their father and dressed by their mother; wooden soldiers, brightly painted, for the boys; and a new pair of mittens for each child. On a little table stood a manger scene, the figures carved with great care by Franz Gruber.

The family welcomed Father Mohr and made room for him at the dining table. They shared fresh hot gingerbread and a steaming jug of cider while he showed the organist the words he had just written.

"I need a little tune for this song," he said. "A simple tune for our two voices and my guitar. Tonight, before Mass, we could sing together, with perhaps even a part for the choir? An easy tune, Franz, like a lullaby, to make us see Bethlehem and the baby lying in the manger."

Franz Gruber looked at the words, smiling and nodding. "Good," he said. "I will try. And you, boys, as soon as you finish your cider, run to tell the choir members that they must come to church early, no later than eleven o'clock. They will be singing after all."

The priest and the schoolmaster were waiting in the church of St. Nicholas when the young singers arrived. "What you have to do is easy," Father Mohr told them. "Herr Gruber and I will sing in harmony, and you will join in on the last two lines: 'Schlafe in himmlischer Ruh, Schlafe in himmlischer Ruh.' Can you do that? Of course you can. Listen."

Father Mohr struck a few soft chords on his guitar. Then he and Franz Gruber began to sing: "Stille Nacht, Heilige Nacht. . . ." It was the first time "Silent Night" had ever been heard. The high, clear tenor voice of the priest carried the melody, and the schoolmaster's deeper voice sang in harmony.

"Now once again," Franz Gruber said to the choir, "and when we come to the last two lines, you will join in. See, how easy!"

At half past eleven, Father Mohr sent one of the choir boys to pull the bell rope, and soon afterward the church of St. Nicholas was filled with village families. They were puzzled. The candles were lit, but there was no organ music to welcome them. Instead, Father Mohr stepped forward and explained what had happened. "Let us sing the old carols that we know," he said. "Then, before we celebrate the Mass, Herr Gruber and I have a little surprise for you."

Franz Gruber led the people in singing the familiar old Austrian carols, which they could sing without the help of the organ. Then Father Mohr came to stand beside him, carrying his guitar. A guitar in church for the Christmas service! People raised their eyebrows.

But Father Mohr's guitar had never sounded better than in the church of St. Nicholas that night, and the melody of the new carol opened the hearts of young and old alike.

Silent night! Holy night!

The Christmas Eve service had never opened so beautifully. After the Mass, everyone said to Father Mohr and Herr Gruber, "Please sing your carol again next Christmas. Let all of us sing it!"

The old church organ was repaired, but it never sounded right. Somehow, by 1824, the money was raised to build a new organ, bigger and better in every way. An expert organ builder came eighty miles to do the work and stayed in Oberndorf for several weeks. He heard the new carol and learned who had written the words and the music. Father Mohr had left Oberndorf for another church near Salzburg, but many people had heard him say, "The new carol? I wrote the words and Franz Gruber wrote the music." Franz Gruber said that this was true. He still lived at Arnsdorf and was always glad to dash off extra copies of the carol. Often he did not sign them. The organ builder took a copy with him when he went home to the Ziller Valley among the magnificent mountains of the Tyrol in western Austria. But people forget. After a while, Joseph Mohr and Franz Gruber were forgotten, even in Oberndorf.

However, their carol was not forgotten. In all of Austria there was no place more filled with the sound of music than the Ziller Valley, where the song spread because of four children. The Strasser children sang like angels. There were three girls— Amalie, Karoline, Anna (called Annerl)—and a boy, Joseph. Their father and mother were glovemakers in a little town of the Tyrol.

Each year the Strasser family filled boxes with neatly packed gloves and traveled to Leipzig, Germany. The trip was long, but it was worthwhile, because the Leipzig trade fair was famous. Merchants came from many miles away to buy and to sell.

The Strasser children helped to gather customers around their booth by singing Austrian folk songs, including a new one that made people listen — and buy gloves.

"You sing like angels," the customers said. "What is that lovely song?"

"We call it 'The Song from Heaven,'" the Strasser children answered.

"And do you know who wrote it?"

"No, it's just an old folk song from our mountains."

Day after day, people came to buy gloves and went away singing the new song. Before long it was printed in a little book called *Four Real Songs of the Tyrol...Sung by the Strasser Family of the Ziller Valley*. It was published in Leipzig with no mention of Joseph Mohr or Franz Gruber.

Father Mohr was always as poor as a church mouse, giving away every penny he had. He died in 1848, owning nothing but the clothes on his back and his guitar. Though he had never expected to win fame or fortune, he might have liked to know how far the Christmas carol from the church of St. Nicholas was traveling and how much it was loved.

A few years later, "Silent Night" reached the northern city of Berlin, where King Frederick William IV had his court. From then on, by request of the king, the Royal Cathedral Choir sang the carol at every Christmas concert. And a letter went off from Berlin to the choir director of the monastery of St. Peter in Salzburg to ask whether this was really just an old folk song.

It happened that one of the monks living in the monastery knew Franz Gruber, who was now choir director and organist in the town of Hallein, near Salzburg. Gruber solved the mystery in a letter. He told exactly how Joseph Mohr had brought him the words for a little Christmas carol and asked him to compose music for it. He described how and where it had been sung for the first time, accompanied by the old guitar.

By this time, "Silent Night" was being published and sung in many languages all over the world. Another Austrian family, the Rainers from the Ziller Valley, had taken the song to America. They sang it for the first time in New York City. In 1863, "Silent Night" was translated into English by an American, John Freeman Young, who later became an Episcopal bishop in Florida. He too has been forgotten, but his words live on in the best-loved of all Christmas carols in the English language.

The words of peace and joy have been sung even by enemies in the midst of war. At Christmastime in 1914, a truce was called for German and British soldiers, and at one point, Germans in the trenches began to sing "Silent Night." From across "no-man's-land" British voices joined in.

In a Russian prison camp during that same war, German, Austrian, and Hungarian prisoners were singing. A Russian officer spoke to them as the last notes of "Silent Night" died away. "Tonight is the first time in more than a year that I have been able to forget you and I are supposed to be enemies."

One Christmas Eve during the Korean War, a
young American soldier thought he heard enemy footsteps
and raised his rifle. He was ready to fire when a group of
smiling South Koreans came out of the darkness and began
to sing "Silent Night" in Korean. When the song faded away,
they were gone.

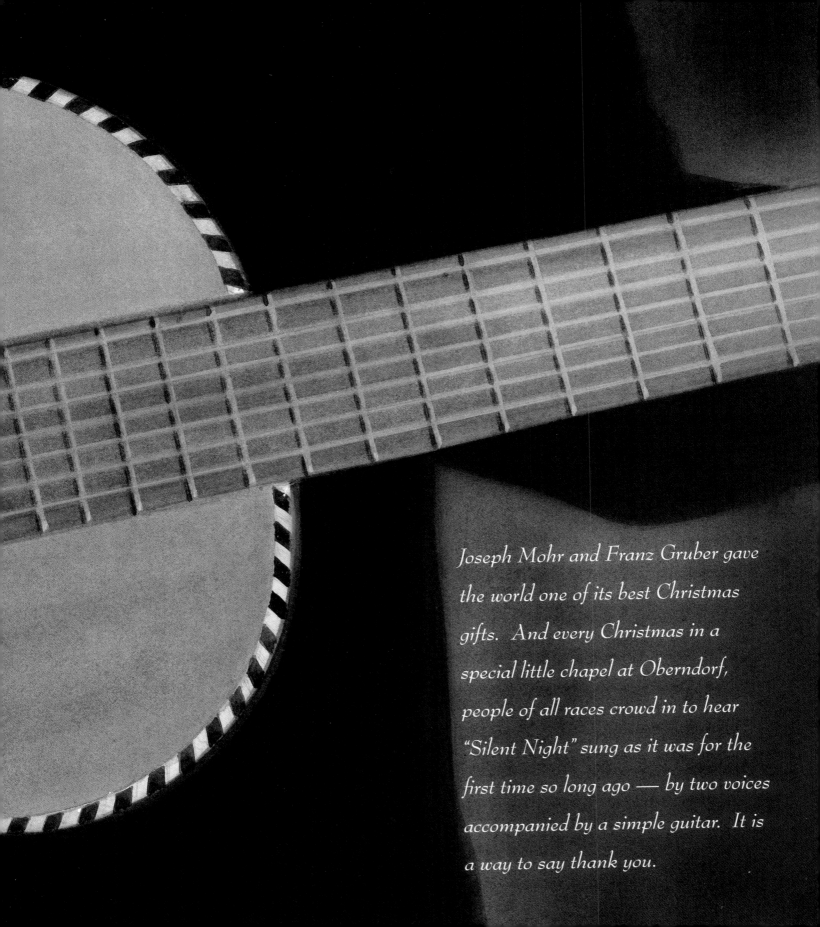

Joseph Mohr and Franz Gruber gave the world one of its best Christmas gifts. And every Christmas in a special little chapel at Oberndorf, people of all races crowd in to hear "Silent Night" sung as it was for the first time so long ago — by two voices accompanied by a simple guitar. It is a way to say thank you.

Silent Night! Holy Night!

STILLE NACHT, 1818

Words by Joseph Mohr
Music by Franz Gruber